Title Page

THE DANGERS OF MARITAL SEPARATIONS

(The secrets to sustaining your family together for the rest of your life)

By

Counselor Adams Kittson-Kotsinya

(The Anti-Divorce Activist)

Outer Ring Road

Accra - Ghana

GPS Address: GA – 404 - 9307

Email: dontjustdivorce99@gmail.com

Tel: +233 548 330 021 / +233 276 949 740

Preface

I believe there could be solutions to any problem that men will go through in this life simply because men (women) are phenomenon entities who can choose a good life for themselves whenever they decide to.
All solutions in this world are there in hiding that a man can find with determination, but most of those men or married partners do not have the patience and the heart to wait for a solution befitting whatever problems they have at the right time to come.

That is what makes some people commit suicide; some choose to drink excessively and prostitute themselves for no proper reasons, and others also decide to get a separation or even divorce when they do not have to. We should remember that, in life, we must look at the positive results through other people's errors to correct the negative responses in our lives for a better life. This is why this book is ready to help you.

To divorce or to get separated in times of marital crisis is a temptation of a lifetime, and it must be overthrown with time and knowledge. As couples, you must know that separation could be the immediate choice if a crisis arises. Still, you must be cautious since separation is also one of the immediate sources of unknown divorces and their consequences.

I introduce this book to admonish you and teach you for life as you journey through your marriage with love, faith, and hope, especially when you are tempted to leave the marriage by separation or divorce.

I recommend this book to a friend, a brother, a sister, and anyone you wish not to divorce or separate in marital crises. Do not present a material gift to any newly married couple without adding this excellent book.

Contents

Chapter 1
WHAT IS THE MARITAL SEPARATION AT ALL YOU WANT TO PRACTICE?

The definition for separation is when married partners or a husband and a wife decide to leave themselves or when they have ignorantly, arrogantly allowed something (marital crises) to come between them so that they cannot easily see each other or do things together anymore.

Marital separations, which could be both positive and negative, can happen on any anniversary of your marriage, and they can also come in any form. So it would help if you were prepared for it so as not to destroy your home and family with it. Anytime you want to take a leave or break from your husband or wife, remember that you will practice separation as a husband or wife. This could bring other misfortunes you can imagine as a family.

Do you want to experience separation or even a broken home after your marriage ceremony? I know you will say no, but only time will tell. But if you insist on practicing separation when your marital crisis comes, please think twice if you are a man or a woman given to quick divorce or separation thoughts.

Just note that anger in the marriage occasionally could make you consider it without looking back. But I pray for

you to reconsider and think again if you want to divorce or separate from your spouse one day to come. You will be tempted to get a separation from your spouse.

Marital separation typically comes about when there are severe crises in the form of violence or any other crises in the marriage. This is when the woman or the man decides to be taken away from the other partner with the help of the court, by family members, or by personal decision for a long or short time until one's bad character is stabilized or changed.

This is somehow good due to the violent nature of the other spouse, but it does not help the marriage to go on again. Also, many of those separation behaviors end up in divorces with time, to the spouses' surprise. However, in a clear mind, most spouses think that their separations could have solved their marital crises, but truthfully, it does not happen like that as they have a purpose. *As you get fond of separating, note that your marriage will end one day whether you like it or not. So, I hope you hate marital separation.*

So then, if you love your marriage that much, which is also a great blessing from your God, it would be better to reconsider when the crisis of separation as a spouse comes your way. Then, it would be good and straightforward to dodge divorce itself if you understand that marital separation can quickly destroy your real marriage forever. ***But by all standards, the best way to escape all marital crises leading to separations and divorce is not to do bad things that bring about the same marital separations between you and*** *your partner for the marriage to stand as the year goes by.*

Also, do not allow your marital crisis to separate both of you for life, but rather try hard through humility to heal your differences as a learnable couple before the court or your family members, that is, if those people come into the issue to separate you. If you do not want the separation, you must work harder to repair the marriage if you have the means.

In my opinion, what I have noticed is that it is primarily wives who get separated. The husbands issue the divorce, which is why the Bible or the scriptures advise wives not to get separated from their husbands when a crisis arises and husbands not to bring about the word of divorce to their wives.

Still, in most cases, the husbands run away from their wives, causing the separation, leaving them with the burdens of the children and other responsibilities they cannot bear. Still, in the state of truth, it is not good to get separated either by being caught up by another woman just like your wife in any way or to ignore the marriage due to some personal crisis you do not like about your partner or the marriage. God is against separation, so must you be if you are really for God.

Solve Issues Than Loving To Operate In Ignorant or Arrogant of Separations. That will help than splitting away as a couple.

It is marital separation causing most of the divorces we see in town today. Most couples will tend to separate from the marriage or spouses before implementing the final divorce. I believe with all my heart that seeing this unfortunate occurrence is not fair or appropriate. And some couples will even love to be in their separation moment for life.

Most of the social vices we also see in our community result from couples giving themselves to separation. Marital separation is all about breaking homes, shifting the destiny of families, breaking the values of beautiful families, and ignoring what is fantastic and mighty to behold for life, which is marriage.

Marital separation is all about you not seeing the beauty in marriage anymore as a couple. Marital separation is all about breaking from history, a lineage of what is valued or extremely important to nature; separation will give you another ugly perspective on life and marriage.

Separation is also about inviting sadness into your family, spouse, children, extended families who care, and even you (the one leaving the marriage for good or bad). Separation is all about hardening your heart and not considering reconciliation. Separation will not give you a free heart to serve God and humanity. You will be serving God by occupation or with pain.

Would you want to encounter one now that you see what marital separation is all about? I will not advise you to practice it today, tomorrow, or even on your death day. Marital separation is all about issuing suicide notes to your once-beautiful spouse, your loved ones, your well-wishers, and even your enemies.
I do not want to practice separation or divorce with my wife, and so I encourage you, too, not to in any way. I would rather die to keep my family intact and

live through my dying than be afraid to save my family through dying and dying later. *To me, that death is not honorable at all.* ***Please believe that marital separation is all the negative things you will encounter after implementing it.***

Maybe the godly sex life between you and your spouse will be cut off immediately, perhaps some of your children will be denied you, and that decision will hurt your heart more than the marital crisis you have.

The consequences of separation can be seen among your peers, colleagues, and even church members, so do not be ignorant about practicing it, too. Learn to vindicate yourself and your family. If I see you separating from your husband or wife because of a marital crisis, I pity your ignorance because a crisis will always wait for you or you at any crossroads of marriage.

Die to save your home and marriage from all that marital separation is all about. Leave your family house to save your marriage from divorce and separation if that family house is creating problems for your wife or husband. Marital separation is all about killing your standard agreement power as a couple. So, kill something to save your home from separation.

Kill that ignorant as a husband or wife, and if it is pride from you as a wife killing the beauty of your marriage, I advise you to kill it quickly. If it is about you loving too much money as a husband rather than your marriage life or wife, try changing the rules for a better marriage. I know it is what we sacrifice for that we gain, so if you sacrifice for your husband or wife or even your family stability, you will surely achieve it with great success. Know what marital separation is all about and avoid it.

Do you want to know what separation is? Then you have a long way to go. Separation is about not seeing your children as and when you would like to see them. Your security as a father would be broken if you separated from your wife through separation. Your children can be hurt, but you will not be there to send them to the hospital as parents. You would always be late in their endeavors, and that hurts badly.

1Co 7:10 ¶ And unto the married I command, yet not I, but the Lord, Let not the wife depart from her husband:

11 But if she departs, let her remain unmarried, or be reconciled to her husband: and let not the husband put away his wife.

Job 36:10 He also opened their ear to discipline and command that they return from iniquity.
11 If they obey and serve him, they shall spend their days in prosperity and their years in pleasure.
12 But if they obey not, they shall perish by the sword, and they shall die without knowledge.
13 But the hypocrites in heart heap up wrath: they cry not when he bindeth them.
14 They die in youth, and their lives are unclean.

Remember that the wisest way to overcome your marriage problems is to prepare for them through wisdom and knowledge while they have not yet come your way. Please do not wait until they arrive, lest you be hasty and make many mistakes when seeking solutions.

Chapter 2

THREE MAJOR THINGS YOU MUST KNOW ABOUT MARITAL SEPARATION

1. DIVORCE AND SEPARATION ARE ALMOST THE SAME: You have to know that marital separation is just like divorce itself in disguise, and it reduces the responsibilities obligated to your partner since real marriage life is supposed to be practiced in one place, but not separate places just because of any marital issue or crisis or even life's challenges.

Remember that marital separations have their prices to pay for taking or accepting them as married couples. *So, think carefully about it before you decide on marital separation on your marriage journey as a husband or wife, or better yet, ask* ***if you will obey this simple instruction or advice.***

2. MARITAL SEPARATIONS ARE VERY DECEITFUL: No matter your marriage challenges as a couple, do not pack your belongings as a husband and leave the marriage, and also do not pack your wife's belongings to sack her from the marriage by yourself, for marital separation is very deceptive, making you think that you cannot overcome your differences or challenges as a couple.

Remember always to give yourselves much time to overcome your challenges as a husband and try to solve the crises since there are no benefits in divorce or even separation at all.

When you leave the marriage by separation, you could also fail in your subsequent marriage, simply because you are a failure in marriage itself, since you run away from your first legal marriage with a crisis.

Or your spouse can even curse you for that imprudent action of yours, and it shall not be well with you in any way simply because marriages are not instituted for couples to run away when crises arise, but rather to fix them. Anyone with the heart to fix things has a strong heart, which means you have a weak heart if you run away from your marriage because of crises. May you stand your crisis time with full strength to conquer?

3. IT IS ONLY GODLY COUNSELING THAT CAN SOLVE MARITAL SEPARATION

ISSUES. SO GET HEED TO ONE: You must not be deceived by anybody to leave the marriage or get yourself separated from your husband for another woman who is weaker or stronger than you to occupy your position (your marriage) through your separation attitude as a wife since ***most men cannot stay alone after their wives have been separated from them and I know your husband is one of them***.

You have to know that if you leave your marriage just because of a marital crisis, it means you were not ready for marriage in the first place. You shall suffer both now or in eternal hell for breaking the law of marriage, but most of all, you shall be called an adulterous woman by people for the rest of your life, no matter how you claim you have repented according to the bible. Do you want this shameful name as a wife or even a husband? If NO, do not think about separation in times of marital crisis.

Because it is only counseling that can solve all marital separations, search for one to help you with or deeply reason with yourself first before you take the step to separation. If you are suitable to find a sound doctrine counselor to help you solve your marriage problems, do not make it too difficult for them since doing that will only complicate you but not the counselor. Never look down on your mother if she is a good counselor during separation. Dear friends must be listened to too; your colleagues at your workplace can also help.

Let me give you a hint. Anytime you decide to divorce or separate while many people, such as your best friend, pastor, or enemy, are against it, you

must put down your pride as a husband or wife and reason to fix your home, respectively. Maybe angels might be talking through them to you, but you are not identifying them because you have been blinded by pain and lack of forgiveness for your spouse.

Ro 7:2 For the woman which hath a husband is bound by the law to her husband so long as he liveth; but if the husband is dead, she is loosed from the law of her husband.
3 So then if, while her husband liveth, she be married to another man, she shall be called an adulteress: but if her husband is dead, she is free from that law; so that she is no adulteress, though she is married to another man.

Chapter 3

TEN (10) SECRET LANGUAGES OF AN INCOMING SEPARATION YOU MUST NOTICE.

Most of the time, we do not see how and when separation affects us as married couples, but the consequences do not differ because we do not know. In that case, whether we realize it or not, we shall face the consequences, but I want to advise you through this book so that you can be careful; perhaps if you see the signs through these points, I have noted them here.

Before the rain falls, the cloud becomes heavy, and before the fire outbreaks, there must be smoke first; likewise, before any marital separation occurs, these signs below must come first.

The Bible says that *the wise or prudent man* *(wise couples see divorce and separation far off)* ***sees evil afar off and hides., Still, the fool goes and is destroyed (proverbs 27:12) . It*** also says for the lack of knowledge my people perish ***(Hosea 4:6).*** This means that if you do not know the signs of marital separations, you shall practice one if the crisis becomes tough or if you are advised wrongly by family members, friends, lawyers, and even evil counselors?

Pr 22:3 ¶ A prudent man foreseeth the evil, and hideth himself: but the simple pass on, and are punished.

Ho 4:6 ¶ My people are destroyed for lack of knowledge: because thou hast rejected knowledge, I will also reject thee, that thou shalt be no priest to me: seeing thou hast forgotten the law of thy God, I will also forget thy children.

Now let us consider them one after the other;

1. WHEN YOU ARE HAVING UNCONTROLLED MARITAL CRISES AS A SPOUSE.

Anytime you see that you cannot control the common challenges in your marriage, you must notice that separation is at the door to destroy your beautiful union. ***Please, the simplest way to control most of your marital crises leading to divorce and separation is to ignore most of the challenges you*** *cannot control and not make a fight about them. For example, if your partner is not changing from a particular character you eagerly want them to change from, it could be the foundation of your marital separation. So, wisely ignore it by not taking it to heart.*

Note that things taken to heart are the same things that disturb the heart. I want you to bear in mind that people do not or cannot easily change like that, but it is God or change itself that changes people, and your partner is one of them. Do not destroy your home with marital separations. It is a meaningless decision that you or your spouse will suffer for it in life. Mark that and know that you must quickly consult a professional counselor in

case you feel you can no longer handle your marriage issues yourself or as a couple anymore so that you can be helped. Never separate yourself from the marriage without consulting a counselor first. You will regret it one day, and note that pastors and prophets are not professional counselors.

Jer 13:23 Can the Ethiopian change his skin, or the leopard his spots? Then may ye also do good, that is accustomed to do evil.

2. IF YOU ARE FOND OF COMPLAINING TOO MUCH AS A SPOUSE.

Please, as a husband or wife, you must read and understand pretty much the person you married and live with such a person according to knowledge. We all hate painful complaining, including our

Heavenly Father; how much more is your husband or wife who is flesh and blood? So, if you complain most often about all issues, especially your spouse's weaknesses and strengths, remember that your partner could get separated from you for life. They may never wish to come back to you again, and not even with the many prayers you will offer to God can save you.

Save your marriage now that you have it at your disposal and never engage in any marital separation, not even for six hours, since six hours are more dangerous to launch an absolute divorce later, especially if you do not like it to happen in your life as a couple.

3. LIVING IN A FAMILY HOUSE OR VISITING THE FAMILY

HOUSE MOST OFTEN CAN CAUSE YOUR MARRIAGE DOWN.

There is nothing wrong with visiting the family house as you wish as a husband or wife. Still, common visitations with some common marital crisis in your marriage could tempt you to stay there even though you are legally married to your wife or husband. As a husband, you must not eat from your family house like you are still a bachelor, irrespective of how you love your mother.

Remember that you have to leave your mother and father and be cleaved to your only wife and enjoy her goodies no matter how it comes your way. If you are fond of eating from your mother's house while married, please stop it no matter how much you love your mother's cooking because it can destroy your marriage later, to your surprise, since you have not left your parents so well that should save you and your marriage. Just know how to visit the family house, especially when there are crises between you and your partner since it has been one of the familiar sources of marital separation and even divorce.

Astute men or husbands will never live in a family house with their wives if there are too many contentions, so if you live in a family house with your wife, as you read this passage now. I will not say much about that. Relocate as soon as possible to save your future wife, home, and family, or even your children, from divorce that comes through separation. Don't be stagnant and puerile to mingle your wife or husband with your parents and siblings. It is dangerous.

4. CAUSING DOWN THE MARRIAGE. If you are fond of damaging your partner for either small or huge issues, for example, beatings and insulting, or looking down on him or her always, or just being a wicked spouse, hmmm, one day you will find out that your husband or wife will go to work or for a family house visitation. They will never come back again, though you are not divorced. Note that everybody wants peace in this life, including the spouse you are living today.

Marital separation is widespread in our generation because most couples do not want to pay the final bills that come with the actual divorce at the court or the responsibilities after the separation, so they prefer to run away into thin air. One interesting thing is that because separation is not an absolute divorce, you

have to search for your run-away partner to come and sign the divorce papers for you to be free. It will be a dream not come true because your partner has gone so far that you cannot even see the tail of them.
This is why treating yourself and your partner in better shape is perfect so that your partner will love to be in a marriage with you without thinking about separation or divorce.

5. IF YOU FEEL LIKE YOU CANNOT DEAL WITH THE MARITAL ISSUES AGAIN.

Marriage is like 'life'; the moment you think you cannot take its challenges anymore, then suicide will be an option in your thoughts or mind. So it is with the marriage crisis.

You must know that some things you think you cannot deal with in your marriage will be the standard for running away from the marriage or even getting separated for life. Please note that marriage is the center for solving incoming and outgoing problems, starting from the children's affairs, in-laws, parents, unemployment and employment issues, making wealth and dealing with poverty and riches, personal workouts, personal issues, and even the separation itself. And so, if you get separated as a husband or wife, you are not qualified to be married again or even for another person to marry you again simply because you are a disgrace to marriage and its ups and downs without loving to solve yours. So stay and deal with each crisis of your marriage without getting tired.

Have you been separated from your husband? Please call out for reconciliation. Are you guilty of

leaving your dear wife because of one crisis or the other? Seek a counselor to consider reconciliation and live a better marriage life after you have come back again. Heal your situation with all wisdom if you can be reconciled as a couple. Do not disappoint yourselves again, not forgetting that what separated you as a couple can repeat it, but you must be more intelligent than the crisis. You must know that marriage is a huge business; for this reason alone, you must not live in it like it is easy to play with. It will destroy you later with divorce, no matter how long you have stayed in it.

6. NOT PUTTING YOUR PARTNER'S FEELINGS FIRST

CAN BE A SIGN OF DIVORCE OR SEPARATION.

In marriage, we are our brother's keeper for as many years as we shall be in the marriage. And so, if you stop considering your husband or wife's feelings, such the pain, regrets, complaints, and even his or her calls or communication skills, you will, by all means, go away one day with the little crisis, or your partner will instead go away for that little reason of not putting him or her first before your crisis, job or work, parents, siblings, and even your friends. Remember that marital crisis comes around the marriage for them to be solved but not to be left for it to destroy us.

Note also that as marriage grows, we tend not to take ourselves so seriously, and at the same time, separations set in. We must be careful because marriage is meant to live for life, not for a while.

So, surround your heart, mind, and spirit to be stronger as a husband or wife, and vow that you will not allow any crisis to sack you away from your blissful marriage through separation, even though there might be severe challenges. I believe it is only through staying together as a couple that you can solve other marriage crises you may have. There are crises in every marriage you will desire to go into later after you have divorced or separated, so solve those you have here once and for all.

7. TAKING THE WRONG ADVICE CAN ALSO INTRODUCE MARITAL SEPARATION IN YOUR FAMILY.

Most of the time, advice, or counsel we encounter as couples encourages us to give up earlier or continue any endeavor. In reality, bad advice has been one of the primary sources of marital separations and even divorce.

Remember that most people do not say who they are negatively. For that reason, if you are fond of listening to people on marriage issues, especially about the type of partner you have or what he or she does for you or against you, I tell you the truth that you shall lose your marriage for the wrong reasons. You shall regret it later because yours was far better than theirs, but you did not identify the bad advisers around your marriage. So then, if you do not know how to regulate your advisers around you in severe and unserious situations, you shall find yourself out of the marriage by separation for no proper reason. And you shall bear the consequences alone while the wrong advisers shall be in their ugly marriages speaking ill about you on their love bed. ***My friend, please be careful not to be engaged in marital separation for any reason; it does not help.***

8. IF YOU ARE FOND OF ENJOYING QUICK SEPARATIONS YOURSELF, THEN SEPARATION CAN STRIKE. I want you to understand that if you are fond of enjoying marital separations as a wife or husband, especially the prevalent ones, curses might be operating on you, or you are just foolish. Why must you abandon your family for peace of mind outside the marriage? Is that normal?

This is an excellent sign of separation itself. Please mark it that if you are affectionate of saying 'I will go one day by separation,' 'I want to be free after marriage or single,' I tell you the truth today, one day these words will come to pass to your surprise, perhaps you did not mean the separation you were saying at the first place.

Remember that what you like is what you confess about, and what you acknowledge is what comes typically into reality, so if you do not want the separation as you say it in your head, then do not say it in your heart or even to your husband or wife. If you are fond of getting yourself separated from your marriage for any reason at all, please allow this book to change you and stay in your marriage and settle the issues that come with your blessing as a married person. I do not enjoy separation as a husband or a wife; some sad stories are attached.

9. IF YOU HATE YOUR PARTNER BECAUSE OF THE PRESENT CRISES, THEN YOU CAN POSSIBLY SEPARATE SOON. This is also a sign of an incoming separation syndrome. How can you stay with something or somebody you hate so much just because of a pending crisis or even past one and still believe you will stay with that person for the next thirty years? It is not possible. My brethren, be careful of hatred because it can destroy everything about us and turn us into separated couples and finally divorcees with couples of consequences accompanying it too. You need not hate your husband or wife because of the crisis in the marriage.

If you hate someone or your spouse so bitterly, you cannot solve the problems they carry into the marriage. Allow your spouse's crisis to make you love them most. It should just be your only child's predicament. I do not think you will easily let go of your only child because of their crisis. Remember that your husband or wife is your only child first before your children or child. LET LOVE LEAD IN TIMES OF YOUR MARITAL CRISES, please. ,

Learn to be considerate in times of marital crisis and consider something else, such as your children's affairs and the love you shared some time ago, and believe those excellent moments will come back again as you work hard towards it for it to come back. So anytime you see either severe or minor hatred in your heart for your spouse because of any crisis at all, note that separation is also hiding somewhere to destroy both of you and leave you with its stings or consequences.

10. WHEN YOU DO NOT CONSIDER ADVICE ABOUT SEPARATION FROM GOOD COUNSELORS. You have to know that the end of everything has already been exposed according to my theory about divorce except the coming of our Lord Jesus Christ. You must also know that whatever you shall become in the future, somebody who is weaker or stronger than you has become one already, and if you are destroying your marriage with any crisis at all, you also have to know that someone just like you have made the same mistake already which you must instead learn from. This is why you must consider good advice to save your home and marriage, and the sound advice is not to take separation as part of your marital crisis solution search simply because you will lose later, even when you do not love to lose it.

Are you going to practice separation in times of marital crisis, or will you try to conquer each one with time, patience, tolerance, and love? The choice is yours today, but I advise you to choose the continuation of the marriage rather than the separation because there are always marital comforts after marital chaos.

Pr 12:1 ¶ Whoso loveth instruction loveth knowledge: but he that hateth reproof is brutish.

De 30:19 I call heaven and earth to record this day against you, that I have set before you life and death, blessing and cursing: therefore choose life, that both thou and thy seed may live:

Chapter 4
SOME MAIN CAUSES OF MARITAL SEPARATIONS

I believe that without something, there will never be anything, either. So it is with a marital crisis or separation, too. Without something causing the separation, there will never be any separation.

We must consider that not only bad stories or bad marriages bring about all the separations we see in town today, but the good stories also contribute to it. One typical example is your partner hunting for a better position somewhere far away from the marriage to better the marriage with the proceeds. It turns out to be bad for both partners due to the challenges of marital separation. Many causes lead to separation, but consider these ten with you. The first one is;

1. TRAVELING SCHEDULES: God made them (husband and wife) two so that they might walk together, stay together, travel together, and even die together. What I have mentioned above are the primary duties of marriage, and not that your husband or wife is lonely while you are married.

Traveling far away from the marriage for your partner to suffer emotionally, maybe lacking sex and communication, is very dangerous, and this can make your partner defile their body against the scriptures or even God. Separation can make your spouse commit sexual errors against you, the one who has traveled, or like the separation through your lousy traveling. *Remember that we usually marry because of the genuine lust in us or the self-control we do not have. However, some might have other reasons for marrying, and so, marrying your husband or wife and leaving him or her lonely will surely make him or her destroy the golden rules of marriage. Traveling often or far from your wife or husband is also a severe form of serious separation syndrome.*

Anytime you want to travel for greener pastures elsewhere. In contrast, if you want to leave your partner alone in a separate mood, note that they are a human being with flesh and blood who can do anything silly with their body in times of need if you are not there. You should be there to handle the sexual and emotional aspects of your partner but not with other persons because you are not there in the marriage with your spouse. If you are fond of traveling often and leaving your partner, it is a typical separation, and it has its price to be paid for taking it. One of the prices is that your love will wax cold for your partner since real love comes through real closeness with your partner.

Also, if you are fond of separating yourselves as partners because of your secular job or fighting, note that it is also dangerous to practice such an attitude in your marriage.

Consider these scriptures if you want to get separated due to your endeavors.

Mt 19:5 And said, For this cause shall a man leave father and mother, and shall cleave to his wife: and they twain shall be one flesh?

1Co 7:1 ¶ Now concerning the things of which ye wrote unto me: It is good for a man not to touch a woman.

2 Nevertheless, to avoid fornication, let every man have his wife, and let every woman have her husband.
3 Let the husband render unto the wife due benevolence: and likewise also the wife unto the husband.
4 The wife hath not the power of her own body, but the husband: and likewise also the husband hath not the power of his own body, but the wife.
5 Defraud ye not one the other, except it is with consent for a time, that ye may give yourselves to fasting and prayer; and come together again, that Satan tempts you not for your incontinency.

2. THE LITTLE OR SERIOUS QUARRELS CAN CAUSE MARITAL SEPARATIONS. One of the causes of separation is marital quarrels of any form. Most separations are the result of multiple quarrels among married couples. So, would it not be wiser to quench any upcoming quarrels that will set separation between you and your partner? I think it should. In that case of avoiding separation, *do not simply hold anger in your heart against your partner for a long time simply because you are in a long-lived marriage life, and that is how it must be for years to come.*

Eph 4:26 Be ye angry, and sin not: let not the sun go down upon your wrath:
Pr 15:1 ¶ A soft answer turneth away wrath: but grievous words stir up anger.
Pr 15:18 ¶ A wrathful man stirreth up strife: but he that is slow to anger appeaseth strife.
Pr 16:32 ¶ He that is slow to anger is better than the mighty; and he that ruleth his spirit than he that taketh a city.
Pr 19:11 ¶ The discretion of a man deferreth his anger; and it is his glory to pass over a transgression.
Pr 20:2 ¶ The fear of a king is as the roaring of a lion: whoso provoketh him to anger sinneth against his soul.
Pr 21:14 ¶ A gift in secret pacifieth anger: and a reward in the bosom strong wrath.

Pr 22:8 ¶ He that soweth iniquity shall reap vanity: and the rod of his anger shall fail. {the rod...: or, with the rod of his anger he shall be consumed}
Pr 27:4 Wrath is cruel, and anger is outrageous; but who can stand before envy?

3. POVERTY CAN BE A SERIOUS CAUSE OF MARITAL SEPARATIONS OR EVEN DIVORCE: Because of the depth of poverty, a husband or wife can allow his or her partner to get separated from his or her family house or another place for a good reason, but most of the results turn out to be evil simply because most of us (both women and men) cannot stay lonely as most people think it to Be.

So, dear husband or wife, in the state of your poverty while hoping for betterment in the future, try to stay together with your wife or husband both in poverty and wealth time and wherever you shall stay when nothing is working for you. Please allow your partner to be there with you or not to be separated because the staying power as a husband or a wife in times of poverty is the actual definition of love and marriage as well.

Note that some poverty can remain for a long time, but you must force it to leave you both so you can enjoy your marriage and life with average money acquirement. Poverty is not a good thing, and it will not make your wife or husband see you as if you are a person who does not love the family or the marriage.

Poverty is a disaster; it could make your husband or wife fall for another person who is a little bit better than you. I know too much riches can break a beautiful marriage, but

poverty worsens it. So, stabilize your financial strength as a couple.

*Pr 20:13 ¶ **Love not sleep, lest thou come to poverty; open thine eyes, and thou shalt be satisfied with bread.***

4. WHEN YOU WANT TO LEAVE THE MARRIAGE FOR NO OTHER REASON THAN TO LEAVE: Many couples get tired of marriage because of its household tasks, so they want to leave and be free somewhere else. And that is one of the leading causes of separations. But because they do not want to be accused of leaving the marriage for no proper reason, they try to get excuses for themselves by accusing their partners of a crime they did not commit.

Still, the real reason is that they want to leave the marriage for separation. *Do you want to get separated because you are tired of the marriage?* Please be relaxed about your intention to get separated because of the tiredness in the marriage, and instead, believe that you will be experienced with your chores over time. If you want to leave the marriage because you are tired of it, know that you will love to marry again very soon, and you shall still get tired in the subsequent marriage. Please, husband and wife, stay together and do not be separated for any reason favoring you today. *Remember that if you are fond of getting separated at any issue, you shall not be experienced with marriage, maturity, or even flourishing.*

Pr 2:13 Who leave the paths of uprightness (marriage), to walk in the ways of darkness (divorce or separation);

Note this as a couple that anytime you want to leave your marriage,

notes that you are going to walk on the path of the darkness of the unknown.

5. HAVING PROBLEMS WITH THE LAWS OF THE LAND: One thing you must know is that you can be a perfect wife or husband, but if you do not also learn how to order your steps with other people's businesses, it can make you get separated from your partner though both of you might not like it. ***Marital separation is a deadly separation, and it can come through any means at all, so be aware always.*** Anything can make you lose your dear marriage and spouse through separation. So what must you do then?

Firstly, try to know who your friends are and see whom you guarantee for in terms of loans and other severe business movements simply because some of the deals you do with other people can make you rest in the custody of the prison yards, to your surprise and that will make you to be separated from your dear husband or wife. Maybe before you return from your separation exile, your lovely partner could have been married to another person simply because they need support for life while you are not there to render it.

If you want to save your marriage from separation, you must first save yourself from troubles, especially from the laws of the land. I know a doctor who has run away from his own country for many years now because one of his operations on a patient went wrong. His family abandoned him even though he loved his wife very much. Avoid these mistakes.

6. JUST ON THE RUN WITH VANITY: Chasing one woman to another or from one man to another will separate you from your real husband or wife you are supposed to be with one day. Believe that, my dear. If you are not content with your husband or wife, you will surely go into separation one day. Be aware always of that. If your character is to chase after vanity upon vanity, prepare for the separation bed.

Chasing after everything in this life means you do not know what you want. Women or men who know what they want in this life try hard to be with their wives or husbands because they know that they cannot get everything they chase after, so they will not chase them with their lives to lose their marriage and family. I know a guy who is so enthusiastic about traveling. Still, he has lost everything, including his family and his wife, who left her family and husband but returned with nothing because she is keen on chasing after vanity upon vanity.

You can have a successful marriage if this attitude is in your mind simply because your partner is happy with you for being aware that you are in a marriage with them. *One wife is enough because the moment you touch another woman apart from your wife, you have committed adultery, and you know God is against that, and you cannot also raise two families apart correctly.*

1Ti 3:2 A bishop then must be blameless, the husband of one wife, vigilant, sober, of good behavior, given to hospitality, apt to teach;
Tit 1:6 ¶ If any be blameless, the husband of one wife, having faithful children not accused of riot or unruly.

7. ALLOWING YOU TO BE TAKEN OVER BY ANOTHER WOMAN OR MAN. Dear husband, you must know that many women would turn to love you apart from your wife.

Likewise, you are the wife, and so, for that reason, you must be very careful about how you deal with your secretaries, male and female friends, and even extraordinary strangers since all of them are or could be the causes of your marital separation since you cannot share yourself into two for all your multiple lovers.

Do you sometimes get surprised that a divorcee soon gets another person to marry them? The world is made up of 'if you do not like it today,' someone likes it tomorrow. This is why you must always love your partner for life since someone is hiding afar off to take over from you by force through marital separation.

Please, do not tempt your partner with the temptation of separation because you know they cannot do without you. My dear woman, do not allow another man to take over your husband with you. Protect your husband through your faithfulness to him. It is a sin, and consequences follow when you allow a man to possess while your husband is alive.

My dear friend and husband, I would be grateful and happy for you if you did not allow another woman to steal you away from your wife. I know strange and ungodly women are good at that, and you must avoid them from all angles and at all costs. Save your wife from jealousy of other women by avoiding separation that could come from you.

8. EVIL SPIRITS OR SPIRITUALITY INTERFERENCES ALSO CAUSE SEPARATION AMONG BEAUTIFUL COUPLES: Most of us are interfered with by spiritual wives and husbands, who usually come through our foods, dreams, nightmares, and evil imaginations, and most of these entities are also the cause of marital separation in most couples.

You can see a husband who loves his wife, but his spiritual wife too is pushing him far away from the marriage or the house to destroy the marriage or the family, and some even force the husbands to get a divorce no matter how long they stay in the marriage. *What a world,* but the truth is that only you can give those spiritual entities the authority to operate through your bad relationship with God and righteousness.

One sad thing is that most couples even forget to pray and fast for their marriages when all is well with them. Stopping to pray for your family and marriage life after your marriage ceremony or wedding is the very wrong way of living in your marriage in the first place. You must pray for your marriage and family when all is well and when all is not well, and then you can resist the spiritual husbands and wives fighting against you to set you into marital separation against your wishes.

I remember when my wife's spiritual husband came to throw me away from my room one night. I found myself standing behind my window crying while he was trying to sleep with his newly wedded wife, and then immediately; I realized the authority I have in the word of God.

I rebuked him, and he ran away and never came again. Be prepared to fight your wife or husband's spiritual wives or husbands to avoid separation in your lifetime in your marriage. Do not leave your marriage to be destroyed by these spiritual entities.

Be spiritual about your marriage because a spiritual God instituted it.

Jas 4:7 Submit yourselves therefore to God. Resist the devil, and he will flee from you.

9. NOT BEING ABLE TO HANDLE YOUR COMMON MARITAL CRISIS OR EVEN GIVING UP EASILY ON YOUR MARRIAGE PREDICAMENTS: *Separation can happen at any stage of your marriage, and it usually leads to the final stage, which is* divorce, so please, be careful as a couple in times of your marital crisis.

You have to know that any couple you admire afar off or even envies have some common crisis they are battling with (it could be something insignificant or significant); for this one reason alone, you must be careful to handle each situation that shows its face up into your marriage and never give up on your partner even if the separation comes your way to win back the marriage since the marital separation is not the actual sin. Still, not coming back again into marriage while marrying another person is the primary sin according to the scriptures, which also his judgment: Roman 7:3, I Co. 7:10-11.

Pr 24:10 ¶ If thou faint in the day of adversity, thy strength is small.

Ro 7:3 So then if, while her husband liveth, she be married to another man, she shall be called an adulteress: but if her husband is dead, she is free from that law; so that she is no adulteress, though she is married to another man.

1Co 7:10 ¶ And unto the married I command, yet not I, but the Lord, Let not the wife depart from her husband:

11 But if she departs, let her remain unmarried, or be reconciled to her husband: and let not the husband put away his wife.

<u>10. PRACTICING OTHER EVILS AGAINST YOUR MARRIAGE OR PARTNER CAN LEAD TO THE SEPARATION ITSELF</u>; we have recognized that it is God who made marriage, and He expects us to live it well because firstly, he madc it *wholly* and *holy* and secondly because we are living with our fellow human beings. Claiming we love God while we do not cherish and respect the human beings (husband or wife) we see with us daily is the highest form of hypocrisy, deception, and wickedness to our faith.

And so, if you love cheating on your husband or wife deliberately, you are secretly creating a marital crisis or separation yourself.

If you are fond of lying against your husband or wife on the most minor issues in the marriage to your parents, friends, or supporters, the more the marriage sets into the arena of separation.

Tale bearing around, gossiping about, being a false witness to people, beating your husband or wife, not giving money to support your family's affairs, and disvaluing your spouse's mother and father are all forms of putting your marriage and family into the pace of separation.

If you are hurting your marriage, I beg you to make a turnaround and correct your errors for a better marital life. All these negative things in your marriage mean you are creating separation yourself, especially if your partner does not like how you handle the marriage's affairs. If you do not consider your partner, love, or understand your husband or wife on non-understandable issues, remember that you are setting up your separation speed between you and your partner.

Also, suppose you do not read and understand the bible and try hard to practice what it says. In that case, you must know that you are also building up your separation with time because you have quickly forgotten God, who made the marriage you are enjoying or having today with its proceeds. ***But all the best advice goes to you for having the heart to suffer for your marriage to succeed. Success needs suffering to make it possible, so do not fear if you are suffering about your marriage affairs.***

Col 3:25 But he that doeth wrong shall receive for the wrong which he hath done: and there is no respect of persons. 2Ch 7:14 If my people, called by my name, shall humble themselves, pray, seek my face, and turn from their wicked ways; then will I hear from heaven, and will forgive their sin, and will heal their land.

Chapter 5

WHAT YOU MUST NOT BE DOING DURING YOUR SEPARATION TIME AS A HUSBAND OR WIFE.

In truth, we do not know the consequences, purposes, and benefits of our marital separation moments, so we approach it wrongly. By the end of the day, we keep repeating those same mistakes in our marriages after the separation and also commit worse things in the subsequent marriage we enter. But preferably, separation comes our way for us to go or return to the same marriage again with our spouses after we have learned something positive in our separation time. But most people turn out to remarry and even marry worse persons than their former spouses.

Some even also spoil themselves with alcohol and drugs just because of separation. And others, too, would love to kill their spouses emotionally, physically, and even verbally. I believe this could be the reason why God does not support married couples to remarry if they divorce or separate, just for the power of reconciliation to be exercised between them.

1Co 7:10 ¶ And unto the married I command, yet not I, but the Lord, Let not the wife depart from her husband: (KJV)
1Co 7:11 But if she departs, let her remain unmarried, or be reconciled with her husband,

and let the husband not put away his wife. (KJV)

It would be best not to do these things during your separation as a husband or wife. The choice is still yours because we shall be judged by what we do with God's will given to us while on earth; if you take them, they will help you for good, but if you ignore them, sorry for you because you will facc the consequences, too, irrespective of your faith in God.

One of the very enemies that block reconciliation is the pride of the heart of the husband or the wife. So be humbled to kill your pride and heal your home from the final stage of separation, which is divorce.

1. DO NOT RUSH INTO ANOTHER SERIOUS OR UNSERIOUS MARRIAGE SO QUICKLY. It is a big mistake to rush quickly into another marriage after separation. It's so sad to see that some even remarry four to nine months after the separation. So dangerous to make that decision.

You will make a mistake because you can't possibly make the right choice since you are in haste to please your former partner that you have arrived, and also maybe you want to be comforted and to be helped by the person you are planning to marry. It is still a dangerous decision to remarry quickly after separation or even divorce. ***Do you know whom you are quickly going into? It is a mystery, so be slow and be reconciled to the devil you already know.***

Know that separation comes typically for us to be joined again, but not to be married to another imperfect spouse just like our former husbands or wives. And note that any person who wants to marry us after we have been separated or even divorced also has some mental problems our wives or husbands have.

Note this: Anyone who wants to marry you while you are in your separation time is an evil and stupid person who does not know God and the scripture concerning separated partners. You must be afraid of such a person because they will leave you later if another crisis arises unless they have also learned from their former experiences with their former spouse. But the sad thing is that many do not know about relationships; they live it to leave it.

2. DON'T DESTROY YOURSELF WITH ALCOHOL AND MULTIPLE SEX PARTNERS TO

ATTRACT VARIOUS DANGEROUS DISEASES BECAUSE OF YOUR SEPARATION. And do not be depressed, too, since your partner can be tempted to come back again if you can handle yourself well during your separation time. Decide to be sweeter after your separation, work on your ***mental health*** as a husband, look good at all times as a husband or wife, and be ready to wait for the reconciliation to your wife or husband.

Remember that all of us love to see good things in our lives, but most often, you can be tempted to activate what you do not have to do during your separation as a husband or wife. So be aware and never make more mistakes after your divorce or separation. In times of severe separation crisis, be careful not to fulfill the obligations of living as a husband or wife.

Pr 20:1 ¶ Wine is a mocker; strong drink is raging: whosoever is deceived is not wise.
Ho 2:7 And she shall follow after her lovers, but she shall not overtake them, and she shall seek them, but shall not find them: then shall she say, I will go and return to my first husband; for then was it better with me than now.

3. DO NOT HARDEN YOUR HEART HURTFULLY WHEN YOUR LEGAL HUSBAND OR WIFE IS BEGGING FOR A SECOND OR THIRD CHANCE TO MAKE THINGS RIGHT WITH YOU JUST BECAUSE OF ANOTHER FAKE PERSON

DECEIVING YOU THAT HE OR SHE LOVES YOU MORE THAN YOUR SEPARATED PARTNER. *Remember that God shall judge you if you do not consider your partner for reconciliation of the marriage, especially if he or she has learned that separation is not good to be practiced and wants to return to marriage with you again.* ***Do not be deceived by anybody because marital separation teaches us many lessons, and your partner might have learned something good out of the separation time, just like Hosea's wife. You need to critically reconsider your separated partner in times of marital separation crisis, too. Hosea 2:1-23, read this.***

4. DO NOT DELAY IN YOUR SEPARATION TIME SINCE THE MORE YOU DELAY, THE MORE

YOU GET WORSE EACH DAY. For how many years have you been separated from your spouse? Is it from one to ten years? If you are guilty, then note that most of us cannot genuinely wait for a very long time without having companionship or sex. So, either you or your spouse would be defiling him or herself with another person, which is adultery in the sight of God. I know a particular husband who mistakenly cheated on his wife, but he kept on begging for forgiveness for a whole two years, but the wife refused.

What do you then expect this husband to do in the following years? Would he not go in for another person wrongfully? He will because you are not there. Please take this from me that latest by one week to three weeks to one or three years, you must make all your necessary corrections and go for your partner, though they might have hurt you in the wrong way, and try to see the importance of marriage or family living together at one place. Please do not value separation since it is a very stressful business and wastes many valuable things from us, such as our children's relationship, love, beauty, and even our marriage success stories.

Please do not use your separation as a punishment for your husband or wife; it is not worth it. Instead, learn to reconcile quickly by gaining much knowledge about the separation.

5. DO NOT CURSE YOUR WIFE OR HUSBAND BECAUSE OF THE CRISIS DURING THE SEPARATION MOMENT, BUT RATHER BLESS AND ENCOURAGE YOUR PARTNER THROUGH PHONE CALLS AND POSITIVE GESTURES. Remember that your children still need parental care and guidance even though you are separated as married partners. ***So, it will be wiser not to hinder or prevent your children from getting closer to your separated spouse.*** It is devilish, and I know you will not be happy if it is done to you first, so do not do it to your husband or wife. Also, remember that if it is well with your separated partner, you can be helped adequately, but if your partner is torn and dirty, it will speak ill of you. It shall not be well with you, too, because we are our brother's keeper in life, and no one knows tomorrow. So do not curse, even though the crisis might be painful and regretful. Husband, do not allow your wife to be separated from you, no matter what your challenges might be in life.

Dear wife, remember that you will be tempted to curse the man who caused you pain, delay, regret, or even separation, but remember that he is still the father of your children or child. Husband, you shall also be tempted to say things against your wife, but be calm and accept that your children need a mother to cater to them, and so if you say or curse your wife, your children too are cursed in disguise.

Jas 3:8 But the tongue can no man tame; it is an unruly evil, full of deadly poison.
Nine in addition to that bless we, God, even the Father; and in addition to that curse we men, which are made after the similitude of God.
10 Out of the same mouth proceedeth blessing and cursing. My brethren, these things ought not so to be.

6. DO NOT SAY IN YOUR HEART THAT IT IS TOTALLY OVER BETWEEN BOTH OF YOU AS A COUPLE. If it is because of the separation, remember that you are cautioned not to marry again but rather to be reconciled and to make errors so you can enjoy yourself again as in the beginning.

Do not use that word in your actions and words that no chance would be given but rather hope that your husband or wife will change and come for you to the glory of God, s that you will not sin against God by marrying again and attain hell later too. When you say in your heart that it is totally over between you, it will make our reconciliation very difficult, and that will affect you so badly and even your children or health. Saying in your heart it is over between you as a couple due to separation will make the word ineffective. Some husbands or wife will never tell their spouses their thoughts about their separation status. This is what they usually have in their secret heart of heart.

7. DO NOT SIMPLY HATE YOUR PARTNER DURING THE SEPARATION TIME: Separation can bring all the hatred one can ever experience. It is a temptation that commonly happens to couples who take the road to separation. Some couples even do not want to see each other again, forgetting that once upon a time in their life, they cannot stay a day without beholding themselves. If you hate your spouse that badly, how can you even consider reconciliation?

If you cannot control your hatred due to your separation, I tell you the truth that it can expand or escalate from you, the couple, and even your children with time. It could lead to not loving seeing your children with your husband or wife. Try to solve your separation differences so they will not damage you or all that concerns you. Hatred will never make you come back again as married partners anymore, as the bible puts it.

As I said earlier, hatred is not good; it will never make you achieve any good thing from your loved one, how much more your separated partner you hate so much. Remember that those temptations of hatred through your separation will come, but overcome them for your good, and never allow your marital separation to kill you both, too.

8. DO NOT STOP SUPPORTING YOUR PARTNER AND THE CHILDREN DURING THE SEPARATION TIME SINCE IT COULD BE ANOTHER WAY OF COMING BACK AGAIN AS MARRIED PARTNERS. Support your husband, support your wife. It is perfect to do that because the children must survive, though they are separated if there is one or some. Support your body (sexually, emotionally, and even spiritually), and give money to your children and even to your wife or husband because before, your separated partner can take care of your children unless he or she is satisfied.

Support with your advice to your partner and children just as it was when you were together as a couple. Comfort your wife even though you are separated, smile at your separated partner anytime you meet, and tell your successes and failures stories.

Remember that marital separation is not the divorce itself; for that reason, whatever thing or benefit goes into the marriage must keep going there for the betterment of the marriage, the children, or even your spouse until

you return. Ignore divorce and separation so that divorce will ignore your family and marriage.

9. DO NOT CUT OFF COMMUNICATION BETWEEN YOU AND YOUR PARTNER, AND DO NOT HURT AND ALLOW HATE TO LEAD YOU. Communication is essential even after any separation and even more powerful_when you feel like not talking to each other again to rebuild any brokenness between you both.

So why cut it off? Do not cut it off; even if itself cuts it off, try to rebuild it by the first step: forgiving your partner for any crime. ***Separation is not good; when it stays too long, it turns out to be a divorce with many consequences.***

Why practice it after reading this book? I know you will be tempted not to talk again as a couple, but you must have an open heart to accommodate your wife or husband, especially if there is a child or children between you.

Do not prevent your children from talking to their father or mother. This temptation is also common among couples, and it makes the divorce or separation more severe.

<u>10. DEAR PARTNERS, DO NOT STOP APOLOGIZING FOR THE DAMAGES CAUSED THAT LED TO THE SEPARATION, EVEN IF IT WAS NOT DIRECTLY YOU.</u> *Do not stop saying sorry to one another, and do not stop forgiving your partner until you come back once*

again. Be considerate and understand that, in marriage, it is not always good to be correct, and it also leads to separation. If that sin is forgiven for real, there is no need to stay in that separation moment for a long time. As you keep on apologizing too, do not bring another man or woman on your marital bed in the course of the separation. It will hurt if your husband or wife sees a pending separation between you.

11. DO NOT WISH TO BE IN YOUR SEPARATION TIME FOREVER, AND NEVER SAY IN YOUR HEART THAT 'TO BE SEPARATED IS FAR BETTER THAN TO BE IN MARRIAGE WITH YOUR SPOUSE.' I want to tell you that it is your marital crisis making you think that separation is far better than reconciliation. Still, immediately after your separation moment is handled well, you will love your marriage more than the separation thereof. *There are always some difficulties in the separation period compared to the marriage crisis.*

12. REMEMBER THAT IT IS MOSTLY NORMAL TO BE SEPARATED AS PARTNERS DUE TO THE CIRCUMSTANCES. STILL, SEPARATION IS NEVER THE END OF THE MARRIAGE AT ALL, EVEN IF YOU ARE NOT LEGALLY MARRIED TO EACH OTHER BUT YOU HAVE CHILDREN. Please think about the affairs of the children rather than your crisis and feelings, and pray for your husband to do the right thing for you as it had been done for other people who did not leave their husbands because they are not married legally. And remember that *being lawfully married or traditional is not a guarantee for a successful* *marriage. You encounter crises in any relationship and must always expect and deal with them. One of them is the* ***separation*** *itself.*

13. DO NOT STOP LOVING YOUR SEPARATED PARTNER BECAUSE THAT COULD BE THE STARTING POINT FOR YOUR REUNION. Many husbands still love their wives during the separation, but they cannot say it. One husband told me, 'Counselor, I still love my dear wife even though we are separated, but I cannot express it to her because of the pain she demonstrates towards me anytime

I pay a visit to the children on her end. 'It's so sad. Likewise, some women still love their husbands despite separation, but they cannot tell anyone.

If you are in this situation, you need our ministry to help you try a reconciliation process. Please do not take your separation too seriously, perhaps when it happens; it is sometimes good to be separated as partners, so try to find the benefits rather than the damages.

Do you know that some couples even separate for them to notice their worth in the marriage and themselves? Do not stop loving your husband or wife if you genuinely love that partner of yours. Separation should not quench the love you have for each other.

14. DO NOT PICK A FIGHT WITH YOUR EX-HUSBAND, WIFE'S FAMILY, OR RELATIVES. ***This is one thing you must never do as a husband or a wife.*** These unfortunate situations typically happen between couples anytime separation occurs, but practicing as a couple is wrong and unhealthy. When fighting against your spouse's family, note that many other things apart from the separation between you and your spouse would be destroyed more. Why must you fight with your husband's parents or even insult them or decide not to meet face to face with them because you are separating from their son? Remember the past of your wife or husband to comfort yourself, and consider the future too not to make more mistakes during your separation time with your husband or wife.

Most people or couples pick up continual fights because they are hurt, but being hurt out of something (marriage) must not destroy the rest of things (family, children, or extended families). Take note if you are tempted to insult, be at loggerheads with your spouse's relatives, and even kill your spouse's relatives after separation that when you are going through separation. Do not fight their sisters, brothers, friends, role models, or careers.

Why must you hate your former wife's parents because you are no longer in love with their daughter? I do not think it is necessary as you get knowledge today. Work on your heart always because you could easily fall into this temptation. Because you do not know the future, you must be respectful, calm, and considerate to your spouse's relatives when marital separation occurs.

15. DO NOT HATE OTHER PEOPLE SUCH AS YOUR CHILDREN, your in-laws, and even yourself as a result of your separation, and also, do not be an irresponsible husband or wife because there is a separation between you and your partner

since it spoils the actual marriage. It is useless to do that, too, and it is also a sign of immaturity and a sign that you are not fit for marriage in the first place, not even a second marriage if you get the opportunity in the future. I have an Aunty who has married four men as a result of her divorce, and she is not talked well about any time she comes into a family gathering. ***It is a shame to divorce and to be divorced.***

16. REMEMBER THAT IT IS VERY DIFFICULT TO HEAL BACK SOMETHING THAT HAS BEEN BROKEN FOR A LONG OR SHORT TIME, SO DO NOT GIVE UP SO EASILY WHEN THE TURNING BACK IS TURNING TOUGH. Don't stop praying for your separated partner, and do not stop waiting until you get back once again because it is perfect and better than to remarry and be separated again if another crisis arises since there are crises in every marriage you shall enter whether you pray hard or not.

But the most significant question is, would you love to get separated in your second or third marriage because there have been pending crises? If not, then it is not also necessary to get yourself separated in your first marriage, which bears the judgment of God if you decide to leave your partner for any other reason than fornication, and even with the fornication, you are not supposed to remarry.

If you marry, you have committed adultery against yourself and your partner and even God. This is why divorce and separation are unsuitable for marriage practice. *Please consider these words during your marital crisis and save the marriage, perhaps if your crisis time comes.*

2Co 5:10 For we must all appear before the judgment seat of Christ; that every one may receive the things done in his body, according to what he hath done, whether good or bad.

Chapter 6

SIGNS THAT SHOW THAT YOU CAN GET YOUR PARTNER BACK DURING THE SEPARATION

Most people will not love to go back to their separated spouses simply because they think separation means the end of the marriage, and most times, too, most couples will love to go back into the marriage, but the other spouse does not read the signs as the couples show it. This book is here to help you, perhaps, if you see some of these signs coming your way as a husband or wife.

Remember that it would be difficult to say, 'I want to come back into marriage by your spouse,' so it is signs that will show them, and those signs must be respected and read swiftly by you to whom it is shown and you have to help out sincerely for the marriage to stand once again. *I will advise you not to mess up your separation moment as a husband or wife so that it messes up the power of your conciliation.*

1. The first point is that if you are not married yet, you can return to marriage again during the separation. It is useless to stay lonely as a husband or wife when you can give yourself another chance to be together once again, no matter the crisis causing the separation in the first place. The only thing that can make you not go back for your separated partner is when your partner is remarried to another man or woman.

However, being married to another person apart from your first husband or wife does not make it right before God. According to the word of God, you can go for that spouse while married to that person. Do not pollute the land that you live on. If you want to be reconciled to your former wife or husband who is married to another person, then the counsel of God must be asked first before it is implemented.

We can see whether one party can allow Sarah and Hagar's first marriage to stand if it is God Almighty's will.

De 24:1 ¶ When a man hath taken a wife, and married her, and it comes to pass that she find no favor in his eyes because he hath found some

uncleanness in her: then let him write her a bill of divorcement, and give it in her hand, and send her out of his house.
2 And when she leaves his house, she may go and be another man's wife.
3 And if the latter husband hate her, and write her a bill of divorcement, and giveth it in her hand, and sendeth her out of his house; or if the latter husband die, which took her to be his wife;
4 Her former husband, which sent her away, may not retake her to be his wife, after that she is defiled; for that is an abomination before the LORD: and thou shalt not cause the land to sin, which the LORD thy God giveth thee for an inheritance.

2. If you still feel you love your partner after the separation, you can call back your partner, settle issues, and continue the marriage for Christ's word's sake. With this point, you must make love run through your heart and mind since separation itself reduces our love for each other, mainly if a new partner is found that quickly during the separation.

This is why you must not stay for long during your marital separation. It is hazardous not to be with your real husband or wife because you shall be sleeping with many unplanned partners if you are not given self-control as a husband or wife or sex tools shall be your companion, or you will just be denying yourself the sexual pleasure of life. ***Take my counsel and settle your home out of separation and even divorce.***

3. If you have learned about the separation itself, you can tell your partner you are very sorry for separating, and forgiveness can take place and, after that, the continuation of the marriage. This is far better than remarriage since your new marriage would also have some challenges you cannot bear when it becomes tough if you are used to separation as a husband or wife.

4. If after the separation, nothing is working for you, for example like, you are in hardship, having accommodation problems, your income is low or not unstable, have no money to spend, and are not getting another spouse that quickly, your children are in hardship, chances are blocked, and having more family problems, you can then go into marriage with yourselves once again because most of our breakthroughs in life, especially that of marriage are more connected with the partners we have as far as destinies are a concern.

Do just as Hosea's wife did to go back into marriage when everything was not well with her when she got separated from her husband. ***Please do not be stubborn about your marriage because we are all younger than marriage itself, and do not be too arrogant about an important institution that can work again when proper counseling is taken into consideration.***

5. If your partner calls you back for another continuation of the marriage through gestures, an apology about the crisis, *a standard phone call, visitations to see your welfare and that of your children or child, and even a smile, you must then give a chance as a husband or wife and make the necessary corrections to continue the marriage because it is far better than to remarry since remarriage has judgment but not with separated* *couples coming back again into marriage once again.*

6. If you have forgiven or can forgive your partner for the crime of the separation, it will be better to think about it, stay back again as a couple, and handle your common crisis affiliated with your marriage. Remember that a crisis is a crisis. They come into our marriages, and we must deal with them until we grow or die one day as husbands or wives. Forgiveness is a choice.

You can decide to forgive or to hold grudges about your spouse. ***Note that what is making you not forgive your spouse is the same thing as making one partner forgive their spouse just for the marriage to be established.*** Do not be hardened when it comes to the reconciliation of your marriage if any crisis comes up. You must learn from the person succeeding in something in life, especially in terms of marriage.

7. If you can bear the shame together, then you can come back into marriage again, and one of the ways to bear the guilt is not to mind what people will say about you for coming back into marriage once again after separation but rather what people will learn from your coming back into marriage after the separation. *Remember that it is tough to return to marriage after the separation, so we do not see most couples returning. Still, the silent truth is that many couples would love to come back for real depending on the challenges of the separation, but the fear of what people will say is their main problem.*

But in all that I say, I advise you that it would be better to kill the shame of you coming back as a couple after the separation than to allow the shame to make you stay far in your separation time for many years or even to remarry. *Please obey God about your separation from yourselves or even other people.*

NOTE. ***Think about your welfare and that of your children or child and not others when it comes to marriage and its crisis concerning separation. I believe those who know what marriage is all about will understand, and it is what matters the most. Do not be like the woman whom I advised not to stay in separation for long but ignored me, and now she is in predicaments seeking help from the same counselor whom she disobeyed and allowed divorce.***

Bearing your reconciliation shame is a sign that you can be reconciled again and will be proud of yourselves. Tomorrow, you did that.

Ho 3:1 ¶ Then said the LORD unto me, Go yet, love a woman beloved of her friend, yet an adulteress, according to the love of the LORD toward the children of Israel, who look to other gods, and love bottles of wine.

8. If you can be an obedient Christian, you can return to marriage again. Obeying God is a great sign for Christians to observe and reconcile. Are you a separated Christian (Christian husband or wife)? Please, your God is warning you today through this book because the bible says judgment will begin in the house of God. The warning is that you should not remarry if in case you get separated from your partner for a particular reason but rather to be reconciled to your husband or wife once again; this is what pleases your God, and you must know that. ***1st Corinthians 7:10-11.*** Note that this commandment is difficult to practice as Christians, which is why it is not good to get separated in times of your marriage but to fight hard to conquer each one of the crises that come to destroy your beautiful union as you see your years transforming forward.

Please, do not maltreat your husband in the cause of the marriage to divorce you one day. And it would be best if you did not also maltreat your wife to get tired of the marriage through your evil ways as a husband. Remember that everybody wants a good thing in life; your husband or wife is part of

those people, and you must not abuse that privilege.

1Pe 4:17 For the time has come that judgment must begin at the house of God: and if it first begins at us, what shall the end be of them that obey not the gospel of God?
18 And if the righteous scarcely be saved, where shall the ungodly and the sinner appear?
19. Wherefore, let them suffer according to the will of God and commit the keeping of their souls to him in well doing, as unto a faithful Creator.

9. If both of you have gained some experience from the separation, you can continue the marriage with yourselves during the separation. The primary purpose of marital separation is to return once again after you have gained knowledge but not to remarry as quickly as possible, as I said in the previous chapters. Are you a separated husband or wife? Never think about marrying another partner; it will be an eternal error that cannot be erased for life even if you ask for forgiveness about it because what you repent from is what is forgiven you by God but not what ***(divorcees in another marriage)*** you are in it for life such as second marriage.

So then, if you want to be forgiven for entering into eternal life according to the scriptures and remarrying another person, you must leave your second husband or wife before you may be forgiven. Still, if you think you cannot, then *Hell* also awaits you for sure since you have committed adultery, and you know for sure where adulteries go.

This is the main reason why you must take charge of your marriage crisis for you to escape hell since marriage

issues will be accountable to the Maker.

Your personal experience counts a lot in the process of reconciling. If you have not learned anything from your separation moment, I tell you the truth that you shall separate again and reconcile and separate over and over again. I believe this is one of the reasons why some couples can separate over and over again with the crisis.

When it happens continuously in that manner for a long time, your spouse will go off, and they will never come back again. Please bear in mind that other problems occur through or between them when separation occurs, which could affect the reconciliation.

2Ch 7:14 If my people, called by my name, shall humble themselves, pray, seek my face, and turn from their wicked ways; then will I hear from heaven, and will forgive their sin, and will heal their land.

Eze 18:21 ¶ But if the wicked will turn from all his sins that he hath committed, and keep all my statutes, and do that which is lawful and right, he shall surely live, he shall not die.
22 All the transgressions he has committed shall not be mentioned unto him: in his righteousness that he hath done, he shall live.
23 Have I any pleasure at all that the wicked should die? Saith the Lord GOD: and not that he should return from his ways, and live?
24 But shall he live when the righteous turneth away from his righteousness, committeth iniquity, and doeth according to all the abominations that the wicked man doeth? All his righteousness that he hath done shall not be mentioned: in his trespass that he trespassed, and in his sin that he hath sinned, in them shall he die.

10. If there are children (child) between you and your partner and you do not want them to face the consequences of the separation and also the divorce, then be humble enough to go back into the marriage with your partner once again and face your crisis together to overcome them for the marriage to be stable later. It takes a man and a woman to take good care of children so that they can grow into adulthood.

Still, not one partner simply because our God was so wise to make man and woman and not man alone or woman alone which He can make one of them bear children alone, but He considers both parties to be involved. *That is why children do not belong to the husband or the wife alone, but both, even if there is a divorce or separation. How can something belong to you when you cannot produce it alone? Is it not devilish cheating?*

So note that the most significant sign to returning to marriage with your partner is the availability of children or a child. Remember that it is not good to divorce or to be separated as a couple, no matter the crisis tempting you to do so, and also, remember that there are consequences to that. By all means, one consequence will hit you so badly, even if it is twenty-six years later.

If you do not learn to reconcile because of your child or children, a lot of benefits will also be denied later. Where you need to sit down and discuss as a married couple your children's breakthroughs, fees, food, shelter, security, and even balanced love **(husband disciplining the children while mother loving or the other way round) (remember that**

love children or child do not only need love to grow better, they need discipline too, so do not allow your separation to grant you one) will be denied by your separation.

Some wives think they can do it alone without their husbands' help, but I have noticed that there is still another man or husband somewhere who assists them in achieving their goals. Some will be on loan for the rest of their lives just because they left their husbands. Some wives, too, believe that their husbands can provide something for the family's well-being, but they have forgotten that the little a husband will provide is still far better than nothing that will have to come out of separation.

Please, mum, do not use your children or child as a cover to separate from your husband or wife. Do not say staying with your children is better than staying with your spouse. That is a sickness and a deficiency; you may not see it today but tomorrow. The future is a mystery; you might even need your husband or wife far better than your children. Be fast to reconcile with your dear husband, my dear sister. Be wise to be reconciled to your beloved wife, my dear brother.

My dear married couples, be wisc to reconcile yourselves because of your children and other benefits you may have as a couple.

Chapter 7

SIGNS THAT SHOW YOU WILL NOT GET YOUR SPOUSE BACK AFTER MARITAL SEPARATION.

1. WHEN YOUR SPOUSE HAS REMARRIED: *The moment you see that your husband or wife is remarried, forget about that reconciliation, and even if he or she comes back, you need to discern before considering reconciliation. This has killed a lot of good people, and you must not be the victim in this year or the years ahead of us.*

It is time-wasting to think about your former husband or wife who has gone into another person's life while he or she is living his or her own. After seeing this, do something positive about your life, and seek counsel first for all that you need. Do not be the type of former husband or wife still sleeping with his or her former spouse who is married to another. It hurts; that is why I do not want you to get yourself into it.

2. WHEN YOUR SPOUSE HAS VOWED TO HIM OR HERSELF NOT TO BE RECONNECTED OR RECONCILED TO YOU AGAIN: *If you are fond of recollecting that your wife or husband has made a vow about not reconnecting to you, then you must be careful to be dreaming or praying about that reconciliation. I wonder why many people can easily break the vows that they had made about not fornicating again, but when it comes to the reconciliation of their marriages, they turn to keep that promise with all their might. But I believe that is foolishness on the highest note. If you are reading this, be wise and reconcile.*

3. WHEN YOU HAVE MESSED UP YOURSELF: *you have to note that the moment you mess up yourself with other severe crises, alcohol, sicknesses like diabetes, jaundice, HIV and Aids, and other messes, then you have to know that you will not get your spouse back again. This is because it is of a couple's beauty that they may wish to go back into marriage with their spouse again, but not with dirtiness of various sorts. If separation has occurred, keep yourself tidy and neat to wait for your husband, and as a husband, do not turn up to be a womanizer because your wife has left you for a while or for a reason you need to fix.*

4. WHEN YOUR HUSBAND HAS STARTED SLEEPING WITH YOUR DAUGHTERS: *One of the expected consequences of separation is that your husband could sleep with your daughter (s). If you are not there as a wife to your husband, your daughter could be a replacement to him against her wish, and if you find out later, you would not* *love to stay with that man again when, in reality, you caused it because you were not there in person to your husband who needs sex at all times. Incest is an excellent sign that reconciliation will not be possible again. This also occurs to wives who have been separated from their husbands.*

If I do not know at all, I know four separated wives who are currently sleeping with their sons, and the day that their husbands would know, reconciliation would be off forever. Separations of any sort have a habit of causing evil future occurrences for most married couples, so why not avoid them ***and be there for your wife or husband for the rest of the marriage through your joint agreement?***

Remember that it costs nothing to save your marriage, only your agreement with each other or yourselves.

5. WHEN YOUR FORMER SPOUSE IS FLIRTING WITH HIS OR HER NEW PARTNER: *The moment you see that your husband or wife is cheating with his or her new spouse or boy or girlfriend on social media or in your area, forget to call out for a reconciliation, because if even that new partner did not last, he or she cannot come back to you because it will be a shame to you or in the community that you live in.*
Do not pursue your man or woman (spouse) pursued by another man or woman (boy or girlfriend) for reconciliation. Always be observant, even as the husband or wife seeks reconciliation.

6. WHEN YOUR SPOUSE IS A MAN OF GOD: *One thing I do not see men of God doing is reconciliation. That is why it is a significant risk to be married to a man of God or gods simply because most of them are too known and heart-hardened. You might think* *they would be soft because they are men of gods or God, but the opposite is rather far. Men of God would instead marry fast when they and their first wives were separated. They do not have patience, and that is a shame to us all. They don't set an example for others to copy. If your husband is a man of God or gods, then the percentage of your reconciliation could be irrelevant or not possible.*

7. WHEN YOUR SPOUSE SEEMS ENJOYING HIS OR HER ADULTEROUS STATE: Believe it or not, *your husband or wife is enjoying his or her adulterous stage, then you cannot get that spouse back simply because only a few can ignore their adulterous state to be reconciled to their husbands or wives. Adultery is sweeter, but sin and sins are enjoyable because they take out the spirit of God from you. So, if your wife has fallen into adultery with another man, note that you have lost her forever, and it is even dangerous if* *she does it openly. Don't go and kill yourself about this.*

8. WHEN POVERTY IS THE REASON FOR SEPARATION: *If poverty results from your separation, remember that your reconciliation will never be possible unless you deal with your poverty. Because poverty can be related to any angle of life, it means anywhere you are poor about where your spouse is not okay with it would hinder the recompilation.*

Some might be rich in money but may be inadequate in how kindly men ought to talk to women or wives, and some too might be rich in how well a husband might be to a woman but may be poor in handling marital crises. I advise you to make yourself rich wherever you might be inadequate if you want your spouse to return from separation.

9. WHEN YOUR SPOUSE SEES THAT THERE IS NO WAY YOU CAN CHANGE THE REASON FOR THE SEPARATION: *This is one of the reasons why reconciliation becomes very difficult to exercise among couples because they want to see a change before considering it, but that is a wrong mindset to have as a husband or wife.*

Genuinely, many couples may want to be reconciled with their spouses, but they still see that their spouses have not changed from their bad habits, or they have detected that their spouses cannot even change for the next decades. For that matter, they tend not to consider reconciliation. So, if you have not changed from what your husband or wife hated about you before the separation, there would not be a recompilation, even if you want one.

If you want your husband or wife back, try to change positively so the marriage can continue.

Reconciliation is complicated to practice; sadly, couples exercise it anyway. Separation makes family endeavors ***difficult, and wise spouses would not wait for their spouses to change before considering reconciliation.***

10. WHEN YOU HAVE ANOTHER CHILD OR CHILDREN WITH ANOTHER PERSON: *Having another child or children with another person can quit the power of your reconciliation or heal your separation issues. I advise you that you will not separate from your spouse because most of us cannot stay without sex or a man or woman for many months, and I do not know whether your spouse is one of us or not. I cannot stay without my wife for a year or four. Maybe your husband is like me, and you must be able to discern that. Wife, do not allow your job to take you away from your husband too often. It is hazardous, and you will lose him later. Husband, do not allow traveling to take you away from your wife* *too often; another man could take advantage of her.*

Separation could occur if you are fond of traveling too much from your wife, and after the separation, your wife can be entangled with another man. You will lose her for life if you want to get your husband or wife back from separation and then keep yourself from sex, leading to having another child or children.

Women, put on a condom or protective pills even if you are having sex with other men in the moment of your separation in the absence of your husband, in case you want your husband back. Man, do not be impregnating other women in the moment of your separation. Guild your penis at all times, preparing for your wife to come back into marriage with you once again.

11. WHEN YOUR WIFE OR HUSBAND HAS CUT YOU OFF. ***Maybe you have not seen each***

other in five years or even more, which could signify that reconciliation is impossible. *This is another point that shows that you cannot get your spouse back after separation. Many have separated and not seen each other again for the past five or ten years. In this situation, thinking about reconciliation is just one (1%) percent out of a hundred percent (100%).*

It would be best to think about what to do next when you find yourself on this side of life. Separation is very devastating and can even send couples far away from each other to unknown destinations. This is why you must not allow separation to occur during your marriage. As a husband, you must not do things that will end up sacking your wife away from the marriage.

It will cost you more with time, depression, inability to take good care of your children, and the evil opportunity to be flirting with your daughters or strange women you do not need to be entangled with.

12. WHEN YOUR SPOUSE DOES NOT VALUE MARRIAGE IN THE FIRST PLACE: *I have noticed that couples who do not want marriage or their spouses tend to separate more quickly than those who value it or their spouses. A wife who does not value the marriage that she is in will run away even if she sees the smoke of a marital crisis. A wife who hates marriage would not love to solve issues about the children and that of the marriage or even the separation. A husband who did not love the marriage in the first place will never consider reconciliation. As a wife, you will beg and beg again, but he will play deaf ears even to renowned counselors and prophets.*

A man who marries you because of who you are or what you have will never give an ear to you if you want the marriage to stand again if separation occurs. If your spouse tells you she regretted marrying you, you must consider that reconciliation would be complicated to establish. Because people do not want to live with things they do not wish to, your spouse will not call you to say they want the marriage back. Instead, they will choose to frustrate you more with the separation, your children's bills, and even curses. She will deny you of the children; your calls will not be considered or received or will quickly be directed to your children.

You will be disrespected more as the years go by in your separation. These are some of the reasons why I hate separation myself. There is too much stress in separation, and divorce makes it worse, so learn to avoid it.

****** My dear couples, I want you to know there is nothing wrong with it if you are separated, but the problem is when you cannot learn to reconcile. The problem is when you can forgive,***

consider, and let go of the pains hindering you from reconciling.

****** There are not too many problems if you have separated many times as a couple. I guess this happens because you lack understanding, and the separation will also stop the day you understand.***

*** Separation is risky, and couples must learn to avoid it at all times. As a couple, you must learn to deal with your marital crisis right in the marriage, not in separation time. It gets worse each day, and before you realize you are totally out of a marriage, the devil will take advantage of your body because you lack self-control as a man or woman.*

*** It should not be mentioned that you are fond of leaving your marriage due to the little or serious provocations as a husband or wife.*

Demons can help you achieve separation, too, so be careful of the devil and those in your family who have allowed themselves to be used by him to destroy your marriage and home.

Chapter 8

SOME CHALLENGES OR CONSEQUENCES OF INVOLVING IN A MARITAL SEPARATION OR A BROKEN HOME.

Many consequences pertain to marital separations, but I will discuss a few with you so that you can learn something from them. One thing you must know is that there are consequences for every action (divorce and separation) us, and whether we like it or not, they will come because we have taken that decision to get separated, and with that, there is no respect for a person too to it. It means that, whether you are a Pastor, Bishop, Apostle, Layman, Husband, Wife, book writer or counselor, and even a Shoe Shiner, you shall be affected if you take the seat of divorce and separation in the cause of your marriage whether ignorantly, premeditatedly, arrogantly or knowledgeably.

Note that many responsible fathers have become irresponsible just because their wives are hurt so badly not to contain them around the children anymore or even the marriage. *Please, do not practice separation if your husband or wife is begging for mercy because of one reason you do not want to accept.*

Be considerate as long as marriage is concerned, and do not hope that all shall be well even if you get separated; it is a deception upon all deceptions, and you shall suffer for nothing. If you believe the bible, then this is what the bible says if you divorce or get separated one day in times of your marital crisis. Consider the scripture:

Col 3:25 But he that doeth wrong shall receive for the wrong which he hath done: and there is no respect of persons.

CONSIDER THE CONSEQUENCES OF MARITAL SEPARATIONS TO AVOID IT TODAY IN CASE YOU ARE TEMPTED.

1. There will always be confusion in your heart and mind because you might think it is well with your husband or wife when he or she is not supporting you financially because you have children with your spouse. That might not be true because even marital life with you was not easy.

How much more is there now that there is a separation and its crisis or consequences between you as a couple? Do not be deceived by any friend that separation is good to be practiced. Just don't do it because you shall lose your good name or something in return for your separation structure.

2. Your children will be separated from you simply because you are separated partners. *This second point is crucial to me and must be such to you, too. Remember that it is always nice to live together with your husband, wife, and children, even if it is a child. It would be best if you did not allow your jobs to set a lousy separation between you and your spouse since it is not only marital quarrels that bring marital separation but other factors, too.*

3. You might lack many things in life since I know you know that two heads

are far and always better than one, even if your partner has shortcomings.

Ec 4:7 ¶ Then I returned and saw vanity under the sun.
8 There is one alone, and there is not a second; yea, he hath neither child nor brother: yet is there no end of all his labor; neither is his eye satisfied with riches; neither saith he, For whom do I labor, and bereave my soul of good? This is also vanity; yea, it is a sore travail.

9 Two are better than one because they have a good reward for their labor.
10 For if they fall, the one will lift his fellow: but woe to him that is alone when he falleth; for he hath not another to help him up.
11 Again, if two lie together, then they have heat: but how can one be warm alone?
12 If one prevails against him, two shall withstand him, and a threefold cord is not quickly broken.

You might not come back into the marriage again. *This is very common among us today, and you must be careful.* Please, husband and wife, this danger is painful to bear because it will make you both err against the word of God for the rest of your lives, and you shall be called various bad names for something you could have solved easily by going back into marriage once again with each other as a couple.

Remember that separation is the preparation for an absolute divorce, which is why the marital court gives a duration of two to seven years to heal your common marital crisis, which is also available to other couples who are not divorcing or separating.

So, if you enjoy separation as a wife, remember that one day, divorce will accompany it to your surprise, and maybe it will come at a time that you do not want, and that will hurt you. Please make it possible for you *to return to your marriage after reading this book.*

4. Marriage is the center for learning, and learning is the center for growth, so if you get separated today, you cannot grow tomorrow as a couple anymore. Please stay in your marriage and heal your crisis because it is better than deciding to leave the marriage one day. *Just learn how to live with each other as a couple and do not sometimes take your marital crisis so seriously.*

5. The marital separation will make you tell your past problems to everyone you meet: You have to know that it is not only you who have issues. All of us do. So, who will listen if we all have to tell our problems to our hearers? I believe that separation brings frustration and depression, and such misfortunes make one talk unnecessarily, even at places he or he ought not to talk. Why separate and bring shame to your home? Reconcile and shame your mockers as couples.

6. Most separation issues are the outcomes of other consequences of divorce. So, do not practice it in times of crisis. If you are afraid of divorce, then be scared of separation too because they sometimes look the same in disguise. *Other dangerous consequences beyond what I have written here follow marital separation. So avoid your marital separation temptations because you won't know the consequences.*

7. Another man or woman could deceive you into entering into another marriage with him or her, and that partner might be more dangerous

than your former husband or wife. This is why God advises us not to remarry if we divorce or separate and also not to allow our marriages to be broken, simply because separation and divorce have serious consequences that break God's heart.

Note that God does not easily hear the cry of divorcees but rather widows, orphans, and the less privileged. There is no scripture in the bible that says God pities the divorcees. So be careful to get separation from your marriage, lest you suffer and later go to Hell for something you could have healed with knowledge, patience, love, a big heart, and most of all, with God Himself who instituted the marriage you have the challenges with.

De 10:18 He doth execute the judgment of the fatherless and widow, and loveth the stranger, in giving him food and clothing.

8. You could be impregnated by another man when you set yourself into the seat of separation because, in the time of your separation, your sexual feelings are not dead, especially if you are okay financially, but being economically handicapped can reduce your sexual drive as a woman, and that can make you think that you can stay without a man for many years.

You could also impregnate another woman apart from your legal wife as a husband if you separate from your wife because you know you cannot stay alone, and that will also cause you for no reason. *Note that men who remain in a marriage for decades have more respect than those who have all the riches but are divorcees.*

9. Other consequences are very lonely; you shall often lack sex, you shall suffer hunger (food) more than when you were in marriage, and you shall be disappointed because you do not know when your husband or wife will come for a second chance in case you have learned your lessons from the separation and many more of marital separation consequences will be occurring to you as the year goes by.

Please, the consequences of separation must put fear into you not to practice it if you get the evil opportunity through any marital crisis. *Note that* just a single separation has ended many beautiful marriages, *and do you want that same story to happen to you? If no, then deal with your marital crisis leading to marital separation, but if yes, demonstrate evil ways of life in your marriage, and then you did not suffer before you got your marriage or spouse in the first place.*

10. A broken home is not only when your home is broken, but it's about you staying all right but not making the marriage work as expected.

11. One of the first things you will lose as a couple is 'yourselves' if you choose to divorce or separate one day. Yes, you shall not see yourselves again, or maybe for life, while you have forgotten that you were once true lovers before you got into marriage. Please do not allow crises to push you away from your marriage.

12. You shall now live in an open ADULTERY if you choose separation or divorce in this year 2023 and even beyond. If you marry another man or woman, note that you are not in marriage but in adultery, and you cannot be forgiven by God, too, because you cannot repent of adultery in remarriage. ***Or even though you can be forgiven, the tag as a divorce cannot be erased.***

13. Your children shall be without a father or mother when you allow a broken home as a couple. I have seen and heard many children crying in the middle of the night, calling them "Daddy," but Daddy is nowhere to be found because of separation. I hate divorce and separation, so hate it with me, and we shall be better people or couples.

14. Emptiness shall be hovering around your home. You will come home, and your husband or wife is

nowhere to be found. Because of this danger, you must not easily choose separation or divorce one day. Emptiness is awful; getting no one to talk to after work is boring, and not getting anyone to touch or hold you in the night is not worth experiencing. Avoid separation after your wedding. Bear this in mind first before you initiate your marriage rituals.

15. Mobile money sending shall become the caretaker of your children, not your husband or wife. And note that money alone is insufficient to care for your children. You must be available as parents walking in discipline, love, togetherness, and commitment and have the mindset of building your marriage before your children.

16. Your children shall be separated from you as a couple as you choose separation, and maybe they would be divided as compared to the children of adulterous women. Remember that you cannot separate as spouses and expect your children to stay in one place. It is not possible in that way. ***As you break the edge of your marriage, by all means, snakes (distresses) and scorpions (children's distortions) will come in and devour you with time.***

17. You may not have the chance to see your children again or as often again. Your husband or wife could take children to a distance, which would cost you more to see your children. Use or set Rudeboy (P-Square's Twin brother) and Esther Smith's husband (Ghanaian gospel local musician) and others as examples. They cannot easily and no longer see their children as and when they wish because of divorce, which came through separation. There are a lot of people or couples in which marital separation has taken away their children from them, and it is not a pleasant experience you must encounter as a husband or wife.

18. Some of the things that are commonly available in broken homes are pain, agony, regret, and anxiety, and you will lose your pride, and depression will take over you. A separation that breeds depression makes many couples or wives promiscuous—sleeping around like goats or dogs. Why must you sell your pride to separation? Seek counsel, please. If you are not careful when quickly separating, you shall become prey to men out there. Note that you are covered by your husband as long as you will submit to him. Avoid the shame that comes through separation.

19. ***Broken homes are not beautiful.*** That is another danger of it. Nothing about broken homes is incredible. Broken things attract insults, and the pointing of black fingers, and those who are not worthy of talking about you will start talking about you and your husband or wife, which is a shame. ***Broken homes that come through separation can be triggered by anything, so be careful about your words and actions in the marriage and learn to forgive your spouse as quickly as possible.***

20. ***Your happiness will be taken away when you allow divorce or separation to take over you as a couple.*** If marriage does not bring joy to

our lives when we live well, many would not love to marry in the first place. Some couples look joyful when they divorce, but that joy is just for a while as long as there are marital crises in any marriage they will enter later. ***Keep your happiness alive by seeking counseling first before tempting to divorce or separate in the future. A healthy marriage brings healthy lifestyles, so you must not quickly destroy your home with your hands as a husband or wife.***

21. Your children might become thieves, vagabonds, and not loyal to you because you, as the couple, have broken your loyalty already to divorce or even separation. I would be happy if you considered this challenge before considering the separation as a couple. Your children might become things you did not budget for as parents at the beginning of your marriage. Note that your children might become liars because you are not living in one place as a couple. They would be taking advantage of you, the parents because you are not on good talking terms because of the separations, and this is a headache and cannot easily be contained by many parents, which typically leads many into depression.

22. Your marriage anniversaries are easily cut off when you enter the arena of broken homes through separation or divorce. You shall start to count your anniversaries backward, and it is a shame to do that if you can learn or consider reconsidering reconciliation as a couple. ***Do not make reconciliation very difficult for your husband if he seeks another***

opportunity to continue the marriage with you. It is not worth it to be too tricky on your wife if there is thought of reconciliation from her side. Give chances, please.

23. The Common or Little help you get from your spouse would be denied you for the rest of your life if you value a broken home rather than building your union. Those help are gone, and you will never get them back. Why divorce and why abandon your family because of another woman or man somewhere? Don't set bad examples for your children to follow. ***Divorce or separation can become a trademark or curse to your family, so try harder to avoid it. Your children will easily separate from their spouses because you are easily separated as well as a couple. Do you want this ailment?***

24. Broken homes can make your husband mad in person, at heart, mind, or even in actions, or to be a drunkard one day. Note that because men are supposed to love their wives, if you deny the continuation of the marriage for one reason or another, you will open up your dear husband to other harmful vices of life you would not love to hear about.

Only witch wives who do not care about what the father of their children will go through in the future because of separation or divorce. Are you a witch? Your inability to consider reconciliation will determine it one day.

25. Your wife, children, and your spouse's relatives would no longer

wish you happy birthdays. The smiles will be gone; you will start to walk in half spirit. The dangers of broken homes are sore to bear. *I wish no man hearing or reading today would be prone to a broken home. I talk about these separation issues, so I know how men and women are broken in town but smiling on top of it.*

26. A broken home will entice you to remarry quickly, and you will still fall into another crisis, pushing you to exercise a fractured again. Second marriage does not guarantee a successful marriage.

27. Your emotions as a couple or couples will be broken if a broken home takes over your house. I hate to experience a broken home, so must you as you hear me. Do not follow your present anger or crisis to deny yourself the future bliss of reconciliation.

28. Hunger could also take over your children if you allow your forceful husband or wife to leave the marriage because of a character you don't want to change to enhance your home marriage or even your relationship.

29. It would be better to seek counseling before breaking down your home to divorce by your own hands or assumptions. Seek advice now because a broken home will make your children abandon you one day. Yes, your children will not see why they should visit you since you chose not to visit them because of the broken home you allowed your home to go through.

I believe wise wives would not readily accept divorce or a broken home through separation because the husband is giving it out. How would you know that your husband is giving out the divorce or separation to destroy himself in the future? Wise wives do not follow their relatives' thoughts to break down their homes; foolish wives do so. Wise wives fight with their last breath to sustain their marriage because they want to avoid the consequences of separation.

They know nothing is good in broken homes, only unfortunate upon unfortunate. They make repairs when necessary with forgiveness. They opt for the best of their spouses to keep the house alive for divorce. They do not quickly leave the marriage even if another woman takes over their husbands. ***My sister, take this from me. If a witch is frustrating you to leave*** *your husband or marriage, please turn yourself into a witch to keep him alive with you.*

Remember that other women will fight you in your second marriage to take over your husband again. Be a fighter for your husband. ***Do not easily let go of your husband because another woman somewhere is forcing you to leave, whether that woman is your sister, your husband's secretary, or even his mother.***

Chapter 9
TEN SAD BENEFITS OF YOUR MARITAL SEPARATIONS.

Though marital separations are not good, sometimes, couples must consider the beneficial sides of marriage to comfort themselves before they finally return to marriage according to the will of God. For you to see the real benefits of the separation, consider what is written below;

1. Marital separations come to assess yourself as partners, whether it is better to be separated than to be together in your marriage, no matter the challenges. Never wish to be separated for any reason or any crisis at all and wish to marry again because if you run away because of this crisis, you shall also run away because of the next crisis in your subsequent marriage if you disobey the word of God to remarry another imperfect spouse deceptively.

2. Your marital separation allows you to make some critical corrections during the separation errors so that they are not repeated, perhaps if you genuinely get the chance to return to the marriage as a couple. You have to understand that crises are part of us, and you and I cannot eradicate them as and when we want to eliminate them. But also remember that marital crisis of any sort has time to come and a time to go since that is how God made it to be, so it does not call for divorce and separation itself when one arrives both now and even later.

Ec 7:14: In the day of prosperity, be joyful, but in the day of adversity, consider that God also hath set the one over against the other, and in the end, man should find nothing after him.

Ec 3:1 ¶ To everything there is a season and a time to every purpose under the heaven:
2 A time to be born, and a time to die; a time to plant, and a time to pluck up that which is planted;
3 A time to kill and a time to heal; a time to break down and a time to build up;
4 A time to weep, and a time to laugh; a time to mourn, and a time to dance;
5 A time to cast away stones, and a time to gather stones together; a time to embrace, and a time to refrain from embracing;
6 A time to get and a time to lose; a time to keep, and a time to cast away;
7 A time to rend, and a time to sew; a time to keep silence, and a time to speak;
8 A time to love and a time to hate; a time of war and a time of peace.

3. Your separation time lets you know how valuable you were to yourselves or each other in the marriage before

the separation occurred. Suppose you cannot see your spouse's little or great benefits while in separation moments, then you have a long way to go to work on your mind. Please understand that common marital tiredness can create other minor crises or more tiredness of leaving the marriage for rest, which could also be dangerous.

Because of other crises in other marriages, you have to understand why it is not good to be separated as a couple and not to come back again with full knowledge. I repeat repeatedly that you should not take your marital separations seriously to affect other vital parts of your life when one happens to rebuild yourselves.
Instead, work yourselves to be reconciled, ***for reconciliation is far better than remarriage****. See it as something that happens to make definite corrections, and after that, the continuation of the marriage must be considered. Note that remarriage is adultery.*

4. The primary purpose of all separations or divorce is to return to marriage and learn to live with your partner but not to rush into another marriage and deceptively think that your present or new marriage after your separation will be better than the former one. I tell you that you shall regret it for life and even your generation to come. It could even affect your children in the next generation. ***So, one benefit of separation is to return to yourself once again as partners, and I know you shall enjoy your marriage for real rather than remarry with many guilts and consequences.***

5. To see the way forward: anytime you are separated from someone, that same person you have been separated from will give you the room either to

continue or not to continue, but as I said earlier, the primary purpose of all separations is to come back again into marriage once again no matter what has happened during the separation, and no matter how long it will take in your separation time too. This is more profitable since we cannot predict people's nature or character, even in God's given marriage. Please save your home in times of real crisis and do not create some of the crises yourself as a husband or wife, and if you have started one already, please just quit it for the marriage to rest in peace, lest it stands in pieces of separation or divorce.

6. One benefit of your separation is to keep on being responsible parents to your children and other things affiliated with the marriage, such as the bills, etc.; you have to know that being separated from each other as a couple does not mean you should both be irresponsible to yourselves, and the community as a whole. With this mindset, you have been separated, which would benefit you and your children. If you genuinely do not want to come back or your family members are not just giving you the room to come back, then you must be reasonable enough to be still responsible as a mother or father but remember that there are more challenges to that.

But it would be better to shame the devil ***(family members, friends, church, your society, and even your enemies)*** and go back into the marriage, but you (the husband or wife) must be the initiator of that reunion since you are indeed contributor of that union as the husband as the head and a receiver as a wife.

7. Separation with significant and minor consequences in your life as a couple will make your esteem marriage more honorable than anything else, perhaps if you return to marriage once again or remarry to another partner with another crisis beyond you. Most second and third-marriage attempters will fight all their strengths out to keep their last marriage. It is a good plan or thing to do that, and I want you to do the same in your first marriage if a crisis of any sort comes. Please, hold your marriage as if it is the last to venture, though it is the very first one, and you shall get whatever solution to your pending problems, even if one arrives in the future.

Heb 13:4 Marriage is honorable in all, and the bed undefiled: but whoremongers and adulterers God will judge.

I want you to notify or understand that it should not be difficult, shameful, nuisance, tedious, tiresome, loss of interest, regretting, painful, heartbreaking, delaying, hurtful, and most of all, unloving to get back into marriage with your separated partner again because that decision would be more beautiful, acceptable, honorable, good to talk about, glorious to family members and the church as a whole and even to the community, continuation from your where you stopped, joy to your children seeing their parents coming back from the separation experimental, judgmental free, something good to write about in your record book as a couple and most of all fulfilling the scriptures in I Co 7:10-11.

Please, I do not say separation should not come; they will surely come because of the differences in understanding we have as couples, but in case they come, do not make more mistakes like giving birth to another man or woman or even dying foolishly.

8. Separation will enable you both to access things well or better, and it will make you both recognize that it was not good enough to be separated in the first place, unlike divorce. Without separation, you will never understand the consequences of advising another person tempted to commit the same crime of separation just like you. So, sometimes, you must enter the separation arena as a couple to learn something good from it. But note that staying there during your separation season for many years as a husband or wife is not advisable.

The benefits of separation are why I said separation is sometimes good to practice, but remember that marriages are not meant to be separated from one another, no matter the crisis. Still, we are human beings; they do happen for them to be corrected but do not abandon yourselves to destroy your and your children's welfare and even delay you in life since you would love to start life all over again instead of a continuation of marriage.

9. Separation gives both of you some ease for a short while, and it also helps you reason well that perhaps there was too much tension when you were living together as a couple. But note that there are also other consequences if you want to be free in your separation moment for a long time. If you do not take care of yourself, you would love to be permanently separated rather than be in a marriage with your spouse; that is if your will is to want to be free in life.

Please note that nowhere is free like that, regardless of your affiliations. So, be used to the tensions your marriage comes with, and never wish to be separated if a crisis arises now and in the future. Remember that crises come to be overcome, always in the cause of the marriage, but not to divorce or to get separation.

Job 14:1 ¶ Man born of a woman is of few days, and full of trouble.
2 He cometh forth like a flower and is cut down: he fleeth also as a shadow and continueth not.

10. Separation allows you to attain some height in life, such as building, traveling to greener pastures, making life a little bit comfortable for yourselves, your children, and your partner, reducing expenses, etc. But it would be best if you considered that, though separation is sometimes good, according to what I have written so far, it has its prices and consequences, and you cannot live without them, too.

For example, if you separate from your wife or husband and travel abroad to look for greener pastures, note that other men or women will be sleeping with you, and that will cost you more without reconciliation. If you value your marriage life and family like your life, you will never opt for separation in any way.

IT IS NOT GOOD TO PRACTICE MARITAL SEPARATION OF ANY SORT SINCE IT IS ALSO A FORM OF MARITAL CRISIS ON ITS OWN.

So, please, do not put unnecessary pressure on your partner and unnecessary marital quarrels to put your partner out into any marital separation so that they can make the most significant mistakes in life later against you and whatever concerns you. Remember that you did not marry your enemy in the first place. Still, the marital crisis tempts you to think that you made the greatest mistake by marrying your partner, so deal with the marriage crisis and not with your partner by going into any separation. Wife, understand your husband if he is seriously against marital separation, and likewise, you, the husband.

But in all, if you do not turn out to understand what I have written so far, I want to tell you the truth that if you get separated from your partner, you will be the one causing your partner to sin against God or to commit adultery against him or herself or even you the one who have left through the separation and it is also you who will be judged according to the scriptures because you left your partner but not your other partner whom you left behind due to the crisis because it is you who left respective to the marital crisis causing the separation which you must not have done at the first place.

Mt 5:31 It hath been said, Whosoever shall put away his wife, let him give her writing of divorcement:
32 But I say unto you, That whosoever shall put away his wife, saving for the cause of fornication, causeth her to commit adultery: and whosoever shall marry her that is divorced committeth adultery.

Please, I want you to understand that your decision to get marital separation as a husband or wife may look good in your own eyes because you are seriously hurt by your partner's nagging character, womanizing nature, sharp tongue, family background shortcomings, and some lazy attributes, none supportive attitude from your spouse, maybe you are not legally married by your husband but have children with him and many more, but I want you to reconsider and reconsider once again that, your partner can change for actual one day just as other people's wrong partners have changed and you can testify of them. Give your marriage crisis time rather than divorce and separation.

My dear husband, Band, fix the evil character your wife is complaining about to fix the home and your marriage. If you can only do the positive things that your partner needs you to change, the troubles of the marriage can be handled. But if you are adamant, then I do not think something good can come out of your marriage, but only divorce and separation with many consequences.

If you have been separated from your partner for any accusation, never give up, but work hard to find the best solutions to build the marriage again rather than remarry. Never forget that marital separation can come on any anniversary of your marriage, and you must be aware of this at all times. God richly blesses you and favors you to understand what I have written so far to save yourselves concerning your marriages and their crises in times of separation.

If you did not understand any of the points I have given above to save your home from marital separation, then keep in mind that marital separations will take many more good things from you than the good things you believe it could give you.

Fear marital separations. Do not just read this book and ignore its contents. Practice what you have read, and you will be proud in the future you did so some time ago.

www.ingramcontent.com/pod-product-compliance
Lightning Source LLC
LaVergne TN
LVHW010557160826
845677LV00013B/3160

* 9 7 8 9 9 8 8 9 4 1 5 2 9 *